The 21 Day Mind Right Money Right Challenge
#The21DayMoneyChallenge

By Ash'Cash

For years Ash'Cash has lived by the creed that says… "Change Your Thoughts, You Change Your Life… Now It's time to apply this to your money

All rights reserved under the international and Pan-American copyright conventions.

First published in the United States of America.

All rights reserved. With the exception of brief quotations in a review, no part of this book may be reproduced or transmitted, in any form, or by any means, electronic or mechanical (including photocopying), nor may it be stored in any information storage and retrieval system without written permission from the publisher.

DISCLAIMER

The advice contained in this material might not be suitable for everyone. The author designed the information to present his opinion about the subject matter. The reader must carefully investigate all aspects of any business decision before committing him or herself. The author obtained the information contained herein from sources he believes to be reliable and from his own personal experience, but he neither implies nor intends any guarantee of accuracy. The author is not in the business of giving legal, accounting, or any other type of professional advice. Should the reader need such advice, he or she must seek services from a competent professional. The author particularly disclaims any liability, loss, or risk taken by individuals who directly or indirectly act on the information contained herein. The author believes the advice presented here is sound, but readers cannot hold him responsible for either the actions they take or the risk taken by individuals who directly or indirectly act on the information contained herein.

Published by 1BrickPublishing
A division of Ash Cash Enterprises, LLC
Printed in the United States
Cover Design by Barbara D Writer
Copyright © 2015 by Ash'Cash
ISBN 978-0-9834486-5-5

DEDICATION

This book is dedicated to anyone who is ready to take FULL control of their minds and money... Welcome to your abundant life!

"Money will ALWAYS match your mind set!"

Introduction

Why are some people able to amass large sums of money while others are broke or never seem to have enough? How is it that some people are able to live an abundant life while others are living paycheck to paycheck, making just enough to get by? Is there a science to making money? Does your circumstance have something to do with your financial situation or can anyone attain financial freedom? These are all questions that have been asked time after time again and the answer is simple... Money will ALWAYS match your mind set!

The truth of the matter is that everyone has a "Money Attitude" and this attitude is deeply ingrained in your psychological mind and effects how you relate to money and abundance.

In my best-selling book *Mind Right, Money Right: 10 Laws of Financial Freedom*, I discuss the 3 types of Minds; concluding that in order to change your money attitude you must first understand the mechanism that controls these attitudes. Each level is important and serves its own purpose and by feeding each appropriately we can become the master of our fates and the creator of all circumstances. The three levels are: the Conscious mind, the Subconscious mind, and the Super Subconscious mind. (For a more detailed explanation on each please see pages 13-15 in *Mind Right, Money Right: 10 Laws of Financial Freedom*). Understanding the 3 types of Minds will help you understand why this 21 day challenge is so important.

"Today starts a new relationship that says instead of you working for money, Money NEEDS to work for you!!"

No matter what your current financial status is, the fact that you have picked up this book indicates that you would like to attract and attain more money and/or financial freedom. It also signifies that you are ready to create a mindset shift that will allow you to live a life of abundance, break free from your current circumstance and live the life that reflects your greatest desires.

This book will serve as a tool that will re-wire your brain and change the way you look at money. Whether it's your environment, family upbringing or societal messaging that has created the disconnect, today is the day we TAKE back what we deserve!

Today starts a new relationship that says instead of you working for money, Money WILL work for you!!

Allow me to assist you in claiming what's rightfully yours and welcome to the first day of your new life!

Why 21 days?

In order to change a bad habit you MUST first replace it with a good one. The word habit is defined in the Webster's dictionary as an acquired behavior pattern regularly followed until it has become almost involuntary. This means that habits are taught; you practice a certain action until it becomes part of your regular routine and it becomes second nature. To effectively change that pattern experts have found that it takes at least 21 days to turn a new behavior into a habit.

"It takes at least 21 days of a new behavior in order for it to effectively change from one habit to the next."

For the next 21 days you will begin creating new habits that will help you reevaluate why you stress and worry about not having enough and release the victim mentality that creates the feeling of hopelessness about your financial future. This challenge is a great opportunity to develop a new paradigm and thought process that will support the abundant lifestyle that is destined for YOU.

How to Complete the Challenge

First and foremost I must confess that this 21 day challenge is in fact a meditation challenge. If you are new to meditating or have preconceived notions about meditating, let me tell you from experience that meditation is one of the best practices to adopt.

Meditation helps to get rid of stress, promotes good physical health, alleviates pain, contributes to happiness, and clears the brain so you can stay sharp and focused.

Your first attempt at meditating will feel weird until you get the hang of it. Your mind may wonder with frivolous thoughts and you will get distracted but stick with it, practice for 5 minutes at a time and gradually increase the time spent meditating until it becomes second nature.

For the purpose of this 21 Day Challenge we will be using what is called Guided Mediation. In standard meditation you are demanding perfect silence and allowing yourself to quiet your mind and thoughts. In guided meditation you are focusing the mind by using audios and mantras, depositing new thoughts into the subconscious effectively changing how you view things consciously.

"It is important that you allow yourself to focus on the money attitudes that are necessary to claim your abundance."

How To Do Guided Meditation

The purpose of using this guided meditation is to quiet the unproductive thoughts and allow a new paradigm to be deposited into the subconscious. This recording will lead you into a dreamy and relaxing state that will allow you to focus on a positive money attitude that is necessary to claim your abundance.

Make sure you're in a place that is quiet and comfortable. This is a two part process:

Part 1 – Close your eyes and follow the instructions in the audio, including repeating the mantras in your head when instructed.

Part 2 – In the note section of this book or on a separate sheet of paper write your thoughts and mantras as instructed.

> NOTE: If you don't already have the audio version of this book please go to **The21DayMoneyChallenge.com** to download it now. Also, This meditation works better if you use headphones.

"Make the commitment to follow through! You can either make excuses or have results… You can't do both!"

When Should You Meditate?

I strongly suggest that you do each daily meditation in the morning prior to starting your day. If time doesn't permit, then it's ok to do it before you go to sleep. For maximum effectiveness meditate in the morning and before going to sleep.

Meditating in the morning will keep the mantras and reflective exercises at the top of your mind and sets the day on the right track. Meditating before you go to sleep allows the mantras and reflective exercises to seep deeper into the subconscious while you slumber.

What If You Miss a Day?

In order to effectively create a new habit you MUST practice the new habit for 21 days. Because of this, missing a day is not an option. It is important that before you begin this challenge, you make the commitment to follow through. You can either make excuses or get results you can't do both! Under no circumstances is it OK for you to skip a day. If you do, then you MUST start over. Our goal is to transform your money mind set, so 21 days is the minimum. Conversely, if you want to continue the process after the 21 days, by all means please just start from day 1 as day 22 and so on.

Without any further ado….. Let's Begin!!!

P.S. – If you have any questions please email us at Questions@IamAshCash.com

Day 1 Mantra

"I clearly see all there is to be grateful for in life. I acknowledge the blessings I have received in my life with gratitude."

Day 1 – Gratitude

Gratitude is the most powerful way to create a mindset shift. Take a minute and close your eyes. Put your hand on your heart and begin to appreciate everything and everyone you are grateful for. This includes the less favorable things that at first seemed "bad" or "negative" but now you realize they have taught you invaluable life lessons. Be grateful for it all because the experience is what has shaped you to be who you are today and what will continue to help shape who you become tomorrow.

As Eckhart Tolle once said, "Acknowledging the good that you already have in your life is the foundation for all abundance." As you reflect, I want you to take a deep breath in and out and appreciate the air that you breathe. Realize that 150,000 people die each day but you were given another opportunity to maximize your full potential. Give thanks that you still have purpose and appreciate all of your abundance that is here now and of those that will surely come.

Mantra – I clearly see all there is to be grateful for in life. I acknowledge the blessings I have received in my life with gratitude.

> **ACTION:** On the following page make a list of the things that you are grateful for. Write them in the affirmative beginning with I AM grateful for…. After you write them down, stand up and repeat them aloud.

Day 1 - Notes

Day 1 - Notes

Day 2 Mantra

"I clearly visualize my new prosperity mindset"

Day 2 - Visualization

Most people know exactly what they don't want out of life and express it verbally every day. Doing this gives power and energy toward a life you don't desire. Physical creation begins with your thoughts and is manifested through what you visualize and then act on.

Abraham Hicks once said "As long as you are seeing "what is", you cannot grow beyond it."

Close your eyes and begin to visualize the life that you desire. Go to the places where you want to live, work, socialize, etc. Use your imagination and allow yourself to see the abundance that you deserve. What is your family life like? How will it feel when you have no worries? What will you do with your time now that all of your needs are met? Take a deep breath and smell the fresh ocean breeze. Relax and see the abundance that is waiting for you.

Mantra – What a person visualizes so shall they become, I clearly visualize my new prosperity mindset.

ACTION: Get clear about what you want. On the next page describe it in detail and be specific. Use your imagination and know that NOTHING is off limits. Dream as big as you can dream. Now on a separate poster board create a vision board with pictures of what you just described and put it where you can see it every day.

Day 2 - Notes

Day 2 - Notes

Day 3 Mantra

"I believe in my greatness and will act according to this belief"

Day 3 – Believe

Before you can take any action you must believe in yourself and abilities. Many people believe their lack of ability prevents them from getting what they want out of life. The truth is it's their lack of belief in themselves that is standing in the way.

Recognize that right now where you stand you have the power to create whatever you desire. The universe does not understand big or small. Whether it's a new job, business deal, or a cash windfall, the universe will ALWAYS give you what you want and believe you deserve. Once your belief becomes a deep conviction, things begin to happen.

Mantra – Whatever you believe about yourself on the inside is what you will manifest on the outside. I believe in my greatness and will act according to this belief.

ACTION: On a separate piece of paper, write down all of the reasons why you are currently NOT living the life of your dreams. Then below write down ALL of your deep desires in the affirmative using I AM. (ex: if your desire is to be a millionaire then you will write I AM a Millionaire). Now, rip up the paper that has the reasons for your lack and vow to NEVER let those excuses stand in your way again. Lastly, read your affirmations every day and night until it becomes part of your belief system. (TIP: Add them as a daily calendar reminder on your smart phone to assure you never miss a day)

Day 3 - Notes

Day 3 - Notes

Day 4 Mantra

"I always have a positive attitude regardless of the situation"

Day 4 - Attitude

Prosperity is not all about money but it is all about attitude. Life can be miserable or life can be a happy adventure... It's all on how you view it!

Often times we believe our circumstances dictate how well our lives will be not realizing it's our attitude that dictates our circumstances. Those who can see the bright side in ANY situation are those who are destined to live the best life possible. On the other hand those who whine, complain, or have a victim mentality are unfortunately destined for doom and gloom.

Understand that how you view something is how it will manifest!

Mantra – I always have a positive attitude regardless of the situation.

ACTION: On the next page write down five "bad" situations that you thought were the end of the world while they were happening and underneath each write down how they were resolved. Now reflect on these situations and ask yourself how did you get by and what were the results. Write down your answer then write what good came out of each situation. Now reflect on those answers. Going forward whenever you are in a difficult situation repeat to yourself... "Everything happens for a reason. Even when it's ALL bad, it's all good"

Day 4 - Notes

Day 4 - Notes

Day 5 Mantra

"Well done is better than well said… I am taking the right action TODAY to manifest my vision."

Day 5 – Action

Now that you are grateful for what you have, can visualize what you want, believe that you deserve it, and have the right attitude about life... How will you manifest your desires?

Having all of the above is important but what is equally important is that you take action to turn your dreams into a reality.

As the saying goes, "Faith without works is dead". Many of us know what to do; but reluctance to take action will slow the process and prevent you from living the life you deserve.

Mantra – Well done is better than well said I am taking the right action TODAY to manifest my vision.

> **ACTION:** On day 3 you wrote down affirmations of your deep desires, now it's time to identify how you will make them a reality. On the next page list 3 actions you need to take in order to step closer to your desires. Each step should be something that you can implement in the short term (starting today through three months). Now share these action steps with an accountability partner that will encourage you to stick to your action plan.

Day 5 - Notes

Day 5 - Notes

Day 6 Mantra

"Today I eliminate that which is worthless to make room for what is priceless."

Day 6 – Space

Scientist have recently concluded that physical clutter negatively affects your ability to focus, and process information.

It is said that when your environment is cluttered, the chaos will restrict your ability to stay focused and limit your brain's ability to process information as well as you would in an uncluttered, organized, and relaxing environment.

Take a look at your home, closet, work space, and any area where you spend a lot of your time. Is it unorganized, cluttered, shabby or all of the above? Your home and work space are a true reflection of your head space.

Make sure that you are making space for the prosperity that you deserve. You cannot receive anything new if you're still holding on to old things, people, habits, etc. Give your new money mindset the room to grow and develop.

Mantra – Today I eliminate that which is worthless to make room for what is priceless.

ACTION: Starting today I need you to remove the clutter from your life. First start by getting rid of things that no longer serve you, then organize your space and notice how different your energy feels. Journal your feeling on the space provided on the next pages.

Day 6 - Notes

Day 6 - Notes

Day 7 Mantra

"I am blessed because I am a blessing."

Day 7 – Give

Similar to the law of gravity that states "what goes up must come down," the law of giving says that in order to receive, you must be good at giving and those who are good at giving will always receive.

If you are looking to make a lasting change in your financial abundance and live the life that you deserve you must understand that the more you give, the more you will get. It is no coincidence that the wealthiest people in the world are also the biggest givers.

Many people claim to not give because they do not have enough to give but it is in this thinking that creates the lack to begin with.

Remember that anything that is of value will multiply when it is given. That which doesn't multiply through giving is neither worth giving nor worth receiving. If, through the act of giving, you feel you have lost something, then the gift is not truly given and will not cause an increase.

Mantra – I am blessed because I am a blessing.

ACTION: Create a "give jar" where you put loose change and bills or 5% of your income each month (Whichever is greater). At the end of each month give the full contents of the jar away either to a worthy cause or someone in need. Journal your experience on the following pages.

Day 7 - Notes

Day 7 - Notes

Day 8 Mantra

"I feel prosperous because I pay myself first therefore I always receive."

Day 8 – Receive

In order for you to be able to receive your desires, you must first be open to get them. Unfortunately many people do the exact opposite. Because of limiting beliefs some stand in the way of their abundance signaling to the universe that they are not truly ready to receive all that they deserve.

It is imperative that we release any limiting belief left in us that prevents our desires from manifesting. Limiting beliefs are all self-created and can be overcome. You deserve all the good that is coming your way.

In order to display your readiness to receive from the universe you must begin to practice paying yourself first. By doing so you are telling yourself subconsciously that you are more important than your bills. More importantly this singular act will allow you to build a nest egg that alleviates the need to feel stressed about money because it will be at your disposal.

Mantra – I feel prosperous because I pay myself first therefore I always receive.

ACTION: Create a prosperity jar and/or prosperity bank account and save 10% of your income before you pay any of your bills. Journal your experience on the space below. How does it make you feel? Are you motivated to keep going when you see your jar/account increase?

Day 8 - Notes

Day 8 - Notes

Day 9 Mantra

"I value my contribution to the world and give value to other people's lives."

Day 9 – Add Value

While on our journey to abundance, we spend so much of our energy focusing on ourselves and our individual needs that we forget the value that we can be to others. Just like the law of giving focuses on the process of give and take, adding value to others is part of that process as well.

No matter how big or small, it is important to recognize that what you do makes a difference in someone else's life.

Continue to work on becoming the best that you can possibly be but acknowledge how your "best you" can make a difference and impact lives.

Focusing on the value you bring to others will help you maximize your full potential and allow the abundance you desire to flow easily into your life.

Mantra – I value my contribution to the world and give value to other people's lives.

ACTION: On the following page write down 3 ways that you have added value to other peoples lives. Now write down how you will continue to contribute to other people's lives and the world at large.

Day 9 - Notes

Day 9 - Notes

Day 10 Mantra

"I deserve all that is good, I release any need for misery and suffering."

Day 10 – Self Worth

Lack of self-worth is one of the biggest blockers of abundant living. Because we live in a society that tries to put people on pedestals, it is very easy to feel less than if you don't look like, act like, or have the things that these idols portray.

The fact of the matter is that you were born with the same power, value and worth as those you view as prosperous. The only thing that separates a person from their prosperity is their thought process and their subsequent actions.

Abundance is a natural entitlement. Your higher power did not put you here to suffer nor is misery a regular mode of living. All of your adversities are temporary situations that exist to teach you a life lesson.

The key to your prosperity is to have unconditional self-worth. It is imperative to keep in mind that your self-worth is not attached to what you own, who you know or what others think about you. Your prosperity is your birth-rite.

Mantra – I deserve all that is good I release any need for misery and suffering.

ACTION: On the following page make three lists: one of your strengths, one of your achievements, and one of the things that you admire about yourself. Keep the lists close and read through them regularly.

Day 10 - Notes

Day 10 - Notes

Day 11 Mantra

"I consciously release the past and live only in the present, that way I get to enjoy and experience life to the fullest."

Day 11 – Forgive

Nelson Mandela once said "Resentment is like drinking poison and then hoping it will kill your enemies." This profound statement is a true testament of how much holding on to past grievances can stand in the way of your abundance.

The more you hold on to an idea in your mind, the more power you give it to be created in physical form. When you choose not to forgive, you leave yourself open to blame, anger, resentment and guilt. When those emotions are part of your life they serve as a magnet that attracts more of it to you, hence blocking your abundance from flowing.

Instead of holding on to a past that is less desirable and bringing it with you to your present, let it go and allow yourself to see people and circumstances in a way that makes you feel good and prosperous. Energy goes, where attention flows.

Mantra – I consciously release the past and live only in the present, that way I get to enjoy and experience life to the fullest.

> **ACTION:** On the following page make a list of the people and/or circumstances in which you hold resentment for and begin to forgive and let go of those situations. Vow to never hold on to anything that does not serve your present feeling of abundance.

Day 11 - Notes

Day 11 - Notes

Day 12 Mantra

"Today I have a clear goal in mind and I am focused like a laser on accomplishing it!"

Day 12 - Focus

Les Brown once said that most people never achieve their dreams because they spend too much time concentrating on secondary activity! They know what they want out of life, but allow the distractions to veer them off course and lead them in a different direction!

Staying focused and NEVER losing sight of your goals, is not only vital to your success, but also to your well-being!

Always remember where you are aiming to go, and make sure you are taking a step in that direction every single day of your life! Some obstacles will try to get in your way, and sometimes you will feel like giving up, but that's only because you forgot for a second what your true purpose is!

As Ella Wheeler Wilcox so eloquently said... "There is no chance, destiny, fate, or circumstance that can circumvent, hinder, or control the firm resolve of a determined soul!

Mantra – Today I have a clear goal in mind and I am focused like a laser on accomplishing it!!

ACTION: On the following page make a list of things that currently serve as a distraction to your dreams. Ie: TV, Social Media, Socializing, etc; On the following page create a plan that allows you to limit those distractions. For example, only watching TV for 1 hour per day or limiting your social media activity, etc.

Day 12 - Notes

Day 12 - Notes

Day 13 Mantra

"I recognize that ALL of my dreams are valid. No matter how big or small I have what it takes to turn ALL of them into reality."

Day 13 – Dream Big

As stated earlier the universe does not understand the notion of big or small. What we manifest in our lives is in direct proportion to what we view as possible and probable.

We must recognize that it takes the same energy and brain power to dream a small dream as it does to dream grandiose! It is also a fact that limitations only live in our mind and if we believe in something it WILL become our reality!

We must stop letting the low standards and expectations of the world cause us to aim beneath our nobility and ability!

ANYTHING that you want out of life can and will be yours if you believe in your ability to attain it! Those who kid themselves and waste time only going after what seems possible or probable are closing the door to a wonderful life that is owed to them!

Mantra – I recognize that ALL of my dreams are valid. No matter how big or small I have what it takes to turn ALL of them into reality.

ACTION: On the following page make a list of some of your wildest dreams. Don't hold back and don't limit yourself. Now, similar to Day 3, write them in the affirmative using "I AM." Repeat these affirmations weekly until you feel comfortable enough to transfer them to your daily affirmations.

Day 13 - Notes

Day 13 - Notes

Day 14 Mantra

"I am a prosperous person who never experiences lack and I will ALWAYS present myself as such."

Day 14 – Faith it Till You Make It

Everything you NEED in life is already in your possession. Many times because we don't see our abundance in our material things we begin to feel discouraged and act according to this physical lack. What we need to realize is that attracting abundance in our lives is not by chance - it is based on our deliberate intentions.

If you feel and act abundant then abundance WILL be yours in ALL things - This includes money, relationships, and everything else in between. Attracting abundance is a direct result of the vibration and energy you are putting out to the Universe. You can NEVER feel abundant and experience lack at the same time. So if you are feeling "less than" in ANY situation you are putting out mixed vibrations and/or negative vibrations that is pushing your abundance away.

Stop waiting for circumstances to change in order to act abundant. It is imperative that you develop abundant habits in your thinking, talking and behavior.

Mantra – I am a prosperous person who never experiences lack and I will always present myself as such.

ACTION: On the following page right a description of the person you would like to be 10 years from now. Then effective immediately, stat acting like that person!

Day 14 - Notes

Day 14 - Notes

Day 15 Mantra

"I am the average of the five people I spend the most time with. I vow to only keep the company of those who can help lift me higher."

Day 15 – Create Your Money Team

The concept of the "mastermind alliance" was introduced by Napoleon Hill in the classic book, "Think And Grow Rich," and is the process of combining like minds in order to create a greater force. Hill defines it as "The coordination of knowledge and effort of two or more people, who work toward a definite purpose, in the spirit of harmony."

Forming a Mastermind group is imperative in your quest for financial abundance. Each person serves as an accountability partner for one another. They challenge each other to set powerful goals, and push each other to accomplish them. Masterminding is about commitment, confidentiality, willingness to give and receive advice and ideas, and the support of one another with total honesty, respect and compassion. Spending time with this person/group will undoubtedly move you closer to ALL of your dreams and aspirations.

Mantra – I am the average of the five people I spend the most time with. I vow to only keep the company of those who can help lift me higher.

ACTION: On the following page make a list of the characteristics you would like in an accountability partner. Begin to identify those who fit the description. If you do not currently know someone that fits, begin pulling yourself out there to meet this person. Start a weekly mastermind call or meeting in person if possible. Also join our private Facebook group at https://www.facebook.com/groups/MRUMastermind

Day 15 - Notes

Day 15 - Notes

Day 16 Mantra

"I know I was created to create and will maximize my full potential each and every day."

Day 16 – Find and Live Your Purpose

Life is undoubtedly what you make it! The joy of life comes from your ability to understand why you were put on this earth, then with every fiber of your being begin to live that purpose!

Those who understand their purpose are better equipped to deal with the obstacles that life may throw their way!

Every road is different, every journey leads to a different end! It is important that you sit with yourself and figure out which journey was built for you! Once you figure it out, it's time to give everything you got to fulfill that purpose! You are here for a reason – find that reason, then live life like you've never lived before!!

Mantra - I know I was created to create and will maximize my full potential each and every day.

ACTION: On the following page write down everything that you are passionate about. Then underneath, write down what are some action steps that you can take towards each passion every day. Ask yourself, What does the world need from you? Now begin to meditate on your answer and begin to put into action what you stated as your action steps. **NOTE: You can never think your way to your purpose... YOU must take action! Also there is no rule that says you only have one purpose in life so if you are passionate about more than one thing you should begin to pursue all relentlessly but just one at a time**

Day 16 - Notes

Day 16 - Notes

Day 17 Mantra

"My power lies in my silence and ability to listen to my soul."

Day 17 – Stay Calm

You can either have fear or have faith but you can't have both! There will be many times when anxiety will try to creep in and tell you that everything is in disarray or that life isn't moving fast enough. When it does it is imperative that you stay cool, calm and collected! Understand that any obstacles or pressure you may be facing aren't really obstacles or pressure, they are exactly what you need to get you to your next level.

Instead of panicking and acting distressed keep your poise and calm! Being happy or miserable is all in how you view things! As the saying goes "When you worry, you are paying dividends to a disaster that has not yet been earned." Stop paying dividends and stay calm! Happiness and abundance is yours for the taking if you are willing to quiet your mind and listen to where the universe is guiding you. Use this day as the beginning of the new you that vows to never let anxiety take over your peace of mind. Remember, quiet time is the best remedy for confusion.

Mantra – My power lies in my silence and ability to listen to my soul. I vow to always live in peace and tranquility with the universe.

> **ACTION:** On the following page make a list of the things that you worried about in the pass. Now reflect on how many of them came to pass and what were their outcome. Now reflect on how much your worry was for nothing. Repeat this exercise every time you feel unease about a decision or circumstance.

Day 17 - Notes

Day 17 - Notes

Day 18 Mantra

"Now is all I have for sure. Being totally present in every moment opens my eyes to inspiring new experiences."

Day 18 – Live in the Present

It is estimated that 150K people die worldwide each day! That's 150K people who no longer can take a breathe! 150K people who can no longer dream and 150K people who have no more chances to take!

As you read these words realize that tomorrow is not promised! As your eyes scroll further understand that when your time is up, your time is up! But also realize that your moment is NOW! There's nothing to wait for! No condition to become better! Simply using what you have at this very moment to create your happiness will attract the life that you deserve!

This is your moment! Live in it! Cherish it! and make it great! NOW has been the only time that has ever consistently been by your side. Show your appreciation and seize the Moment! You only have one live to live!! Live it NOW! Live it right!!

Mantra – Now is all I have for sure. Being totally present in every moment opens my eyes to inspiring new experiences.

ACTION: Think about the next 24 hours. If this was the only time you had left what are some task if left undone would you regret not doing. Now. on the following page make a list of the action steps that need to be done in order to begin accomplishing these task. Begin immediately implementing these action steps. Repeat this activity any time you start living too much in the future .

Day 18 - Notes

Day 18 - Notes

Day 19 Mantra

"Every day I stop and look around and realize my life is pretty amazing."

Day 19 – Reflection

Now that you have this new mind set look at your space (home, work, etc). Does this reflect your new prosperous thoughts? Remember that what you see on the outside is a direct reflection on what you feel on the inside. Have you now realized how good you already have it?

Oprah once said "The more you praise and celebrate your life, the more there is in life to celebrate. Make sure that while you are on your journey you are stopping to smell the roses. Look at the scenery, eat the fruits of your labor and simply celebrate exactly who you are right now.

Take a moment to reflect. Be proud of your accomplishments. Get excited at how far you have come and know that you haven't come this far to only come this far.

Mantra – Every day I stop and look around and realize my life is pretty amazing.

ACTION: Go to the gratitude list that you created on day one and reflect on all of the things that you are grateful for. Sit and meditate on how good your life really is and simply say thank you for all that you have right now.

Day 19 - Notes

Day 19 - Notes

Day 20 Mantra

"I am tenacious in my commitment to change my money mind set and ultimately change my life."

Day 20 – Commit

Commitment means staying loyal to what you said you were going to do long after the mood you said it in has left. Many times we make the grave mistake of being satisfied with our intentions. We think that because we intend to do something that it is enough to help us actually attain it. While intent reveals your desires, only action can reveal your commitment!

If you truly believe something, you will attempt to live it no matter what. Effective immediately you must have an unwavering commitment to make your dreams happen.

To that end, changing your money mind set MUST be a commitment and what you have learned so far and will continue to learn MUST be practiced and applied.

Let today be the day that you become committed to your dreams and aspirations, let today be the day you commit to doing what it takes to make them come true and let today be the day you vow to get, achieve, and experience the life of your dreams!

Mantra – I am tenacious in my commitment to change my money mindset and ultimately change my life.

ACTION: Think about how you want your finances to look then on the following page rewrite them in the affirmative starting with the words "I am committed to…"

Day 20 - Notes

Day 20 - Notes

Day 21 Mantra

"I am refreshed, rejuvenated, and reborn. I will continue to live my life abundantly the way it was divinely meant."

Day 21 – Completion/Rebirth?

Every ending starts something new and as the creator of your life's story it is imperative that you end the story you don't want and replace it with a new story that fits your desires!

Many times our unwillingness to let go of struggle is the only reason why our life isn't the way we want it to be.

Now that you have reached day 21 and well on your way to solidifying your new mind set, it is time to continue to let go of who you were in order to fully become who you want and need to be.

Today marks the official first day of your new life. Whatever went wrong in the past should stay there! Learn what was taught but now is the time to move on and start anew! Remember: Pace yourself. Life is a marathon not a sprint! Don't get so caught up in the momentum of this new beginning that you burn yourself out! Enjoy the ride and don't rush. There is no destination just the journey.

Mantra – I am refreshed, rejuvenated, and reborn. I will continue to live my life abundantly the way it was divinely meant.

> **ACTION:** On the following page journal your thoughts on this 21 day challenge and list how has it change the way you view money. Also visit our private Facebook mastermind group to share your thoughts with others.

Day 21 - Notes

Day 21 - Notes

"Wherever you are right now is where you are and where you should begin!"

Epilogue

Thank you for completing the 21 day Mind Right, Money Right Challenge. Your commitment is applauded and the fruits of your labor will surely begin to sprout.

As you continue on your journey towards financial freedom, you must realize that your story is your story and your path is your path! Often times people put time limits on their success and want everything to be the way its "supposed" to be by a certain time-frame.

We tend to look at others who may seem to have everything together and wish that our own life was similar. What we need to realize as soon as possible is that on the road to success time doesn't matter!

Who cares how long it takes to get to your destination as long as you get there! Progress is progress no matter what. Stop worrying about what others think or what others are doing! Their path is their path and yours is yours! No two people will ever have the same story so it is ridiculous to even look and compare yours with those of others.

Wherever you are right now is where you are and where you should begin! Close a blind eye to what others are doing and simply do your best!

"Today and every day starts the first day of the rest of your life. What you decide to do with it will determine whether you live a life of abundance or do you live mediocre... Choose wisely!"

As Romana Anderson once said "People spend a lifetime searching for happiness; looking for peace. They chase idle dreams, addictions, religions, even other people, hoping to fill the emptiness that plagues them. The irony is the only place they ever needed to search was within." Look inside, run your race, and Succeed at Your Own Pace!

It is highly suggested that you continue to do the 21 day challenge as many times as needed in order to solidify your new money mindset.

After you feel comfortable, it is again highly suggested that you keep meditation as a daily practice and routine. In the next few pages you will be given a guide on how to properly meditate as well as a list of affirmations that you can use to recharge yourself.

Today and every day starts the first day of the rest of your life. What you decide to do with it will determine whether you live a life of abundance or do you live mediocre. .. Choose wisely!

There is no better time than NOW to begin living the life that you deserve. #NothingCanStopYOUbutYOU!

One love,

Ash'Cash

Ash'Cash

Meditation 101

Here are some simple tips on how to meditate.

I - Practice Good Posture

You can choose to either sit on a chair or on the floor with your legs crossed. Make sure that your spine is upright with your head up. Your mind and body are intertwined so if you are slumped your mind will drift. A well-balanced body equals a well-balanced mind. To straighten up, imagine that your head is touching the sky. Note: Laying in the bed or on your back is not recommended.

II - Keep Your Eyes Open (If you can)

Do your best to keep your eyes open. To do so just lower your eyes and let your gaze be soft. By keeping your eyes opened it will allow you to be more present. Keeping your eyes closed is an option but doing so usually makes it more likely for your mind to drift away. Many people prefer to close their eyes so by all means do what makes you comfortable. It's a good idea to experiment with both to see what is most effective.

III – Monitor Your Breathing

Paying attention to how you breath is a great way to anchor yourself in the present moment. Pay attention to how your breath is streaming in and out. Don't focus too much on how you are breathing – just let it be natural. If you find that your mind is straying, you can also try counting your breath – which is an ancient meditation practice. On your outbreath, silently count "one", then "two", and up to "four". Then return to "one".

IV - Find a Mantra (If necessary)

In some cases monitoring or counting your breathe may not work for you. In that case I recommend using a mantra. A mantra is a word, sound, or phrase that you repeat to yourself in order to aid in your concentration while meditating. A mantra can be as simple as the sound 'rum' or word 'love,' It can be something you are thankful for or an affirmation, such as 'I accept myself.' Sometimes choosing a sound that can be stripped of all meaning works best because it won't bring up any connotation, interpretation or judgment when you hear It.

V – Let Your Thoughts Go…

When you notice your thoughts, gently let them go by returning your focus to your breathing or your mantra. Don't try to stop the thoughts because this will just make you feel agitated and defeat the purpose of meditation. Simply acknowledge the presence of these thoughts and calmly let them go.

VI- Start with 10 Minutes…

Some people enjoy meditating for an hour at a time while others find that they can't sit longer than 10 minutes. When you first begin it's important that you do what feels right for you. Start with 10 minutes and only sit longer if you feel like 10 minutes is too short. Don't force yourself to meditate longer if you are not ready to do that. Some may also find setting an alarm useful. Setting your alarm for 10 or 20 minutes will allow you to not worry about the time hence lettng your mind relax.

VII – Create a relaxing atmosphere…

If possible create a special place to sit while you meditate. Some people have created a shrine or an altar that they face during meditation. If you don't want to go that far just yet, you can start small by placing a candle in front of you or objects that has meaning to you.

VIII – Enjoy yourself...

The most important part of meditation is that you enjoy yourself. Try smiling as you meditate. Be kind to yourself and enjoy your peace of mind.

Books on Meditation

1. *Success Through Stillness: Meditation Made Simple* By Russell Simmons
2. *Zen Mind, Beginner's Mind* by Suzuki Roshi
3. *A Path With Heart* by Jack Kornfield
4. *Wherever you go, there you are* by John Kabat-Zinn, Ph.D
5. *Open Heart, Open Mind* by Tsoknyi Rinpoche
6. *Loving-Kindness* by Sharon Salzberg
7. *The Miracle of Mindfulness: An Introduction to the Practice of Meditation,* By Thich Nhat Hanh
8. *Mindfulness in Plain English,* By Bhante Gunaratana
9. *Cutting Through Spiritual Materialism,* By Chogam Trung
10. *The Power of Now: A Guide to Spiritual Enlightenment* by Eckhart Tolle

Affirmations

- When my why is strong enough, my how always appears.

- I follow my bliss. I experience my bliss. I am my bliss.

- I am absolutely committed to being the person I came to the planet to be!

- I will accomplish great things. One by one, I am achieving all of them!

- I have a clear goal in mind and I am focused like a laser on accomplishing it!

- Today I block out distractions and remain committed to my tasks!

- I am turning my goals into action and my actions into results.

- When I set out to achieve something I eliminate all the negatives and naysayers and focus completely on my goal!

- Everything that happens in my life perfectly prepares me to achieve my dreams!

- I am at the top of my game. I have unstoppable momentum all the way to my dreams!

- My life is a testament to the power of determination. When I go the extra mile success is always waiting.

- I pay attention to what is most important to me and I pursue that relentlessly!

- I live with purpose and my purpose lights my path to my goals and dreams!

- I take committed action for my dreams. I am on the fast track to them right now!

- My purpose is clear and the path to achieving my dreams is opening before me.

- I am ready for whatever challenges life brings today. Nothing can stop me! I am pushing forward towards my goals.

- Empowered thoughts and determined action are manifesting my dreams faster than ever today!

- I think power thoughts! I take power action! I achieve power results!

- My goals are right in front of me. Today I'm all about achieving them!

- Today my believing becomes achieving, as my actions turn to results.

- I am blowing by my limitations and achieving my most cherished dreams.

- Today I am digging deep, reaching high, and achieving great things!

- I left my doubts in the dust and I am climbing the mountain of my dreams!

- Today I convert my potential into action and results!

- I am pushing through my barriers and on to bigger and better things.

- I push my limits and I achieve great things!

- Every giant achievement was once a small dream acted upon. Today I act on my dreams!

- Today I spend more energy on my goals than on my worries!

- I release every attachment that holds me back from my goals and pursue my dreams with determination!

- I give myself completely to my purpose and my purpose gives me completely to success and happiness.

- Today I remember that every situation is part of my purpose and my plan coming together perfectly!

- I AM HERE. And if I am here, I am here for a reason.

- Today and every day, all the pieces are falling together perfectly in my life.

About the Author

Ash Exantus aka Ash Cash is a speaker, bestselling author, business consultant, and spiritual adviser to entrepreneurs, celebrities, athletes, and executives

Ash has been featured on popular, national media outlets such as CNN, The New York Times, WSJ, American Banker, CNBC, TheStreet.com, Black Enterprise, Essence Magazine, Ebony, BET, Pix11 Morning News, Fox Business News, and countless others.

For those of you interested in the possibility of Life or Business Coaching From Ash, contact him though his website www.IamAshCash.com

www.ingramcontent.com/pod-product-compliance
Lightning Source LLC
LaVergne TN
LVHW020327080426
835507LV00036BA/3318